Forgiveness

Healing

Restoration

Unfolding Truths of how God led me through the process of healing in every aspect of my life. Holding on to God's promises through every obstacle in our lives is a necessity. He is the same yesterday, today, and forever. He knew our need for Him and His promises before we knew we had need of Him.

Forgiveness

 Healing

Restoration

Copyright @ 2022 by:

HopeBlessingsPublication

Edited by: Hope White and Rebecca Bratton

Printed by: KDP by Amazon. USA

ISBN: 979-8-88722-245-5

Table of Content

Dedication

I want to dedicate this book to my husband Carlos and our children David and Serena. I pray that you will apply these Godly principles to your everyday lives and make living for Jesus your lifestyle.

I want to dedicate this book to my parents Gary and Lola Worthen. Thank you for instilling these same principles into my life, along with my seven siblings. We are eternally grateful for the time and prayer invested into our lives.

Preface

I have read books on forgiveness, healing and personal development that have helped me in many ways but reading and studying God's Word is my turning point in everything.

God's Word is the blueprint for everything. It covers every important topic concerning life and teaches us how to become like Christ. It is character building and will shape us into who He wants. It will guide us step by step through the process to achieve a solid foundation and make living for God a lifestyle. Therefore, I began drafting this book over a year ago. I had accumulated notes throughout my process of forgiveness, healing, and restoration. Much of my knowledge is from having my own experiences and applying what I have learn from God's Word. I will be suggesting to all my readers to read God's Word daily. Allow it to become a blueprint to build Godly Characteristics and a road map to guide our steps.

Psalms 119:105 "Thy Word is
a lamp unto my feet, and a light
unto my path."

Introduction

This book is about truths of forgiveness, healing, and restoration in my life and how God helped me. My desire is to throw out a lifeline to bring those that are drowning in pain, hurts and unfortunate situations to a safe place within God's reassuring love and grace.

I want to help you find yourself, your uniqueness, your value, your purpose, and your worth in God.

In these pages I will share my journey of these unfolding truths in my life and how I had to rely on God. We all go through times where we must decide to learn from our experiences and trials of life or to give into them and allow them to control who we are. Sometimes we get answers to why we went through those trials; other times we may never get the closure we want. We must learn how to keep self-control, learn from what we go through, and that our response reflects our character, who we stand for and affects those around us.

I went through things that cut to the core of my very being, but I had to choose what my response would be. I knew that my response would decide the person I would become and where it could lead me. I would love to say that my responses were all perfect; however, there is none perfect except Jesus Christ. It is only through Him that we can have the perfect response. I had to learn to choose better responses and what best helped me get through those hard challenging days. The purpose of this book is to help those that go through things you simply do not understand and have even said, "Why me, God?" I will be sharing my thoughts, hurts and responses in a way that can relate to our human emotions, but I am in no way pointing fingers, neither is this written to downgrade or demoralize those that have hurt me. It is solely to give you a peek into human/spiritual emotions on how we should and should not respond to the hurts, pains, and obstacles of life according to God's Word.

I have often asked myself; how can I affect the world and why am I not doing so? I began to do serious soul searching, I realized I needed to:

- Know that I am a child of the Highest King.
- Know who I am and my purpose in Him.
- Know my value.
- Know my beliefs.
- Know why I believe them.
- Know where I am going.
- Know why I am going there.
- Know the Biblical plan on how to get there.
- Know that I may not know when, but that I will get there.

- Know that whatever it is, I have determined to do, that it is bigger than me.
- Stay true to God, Myself, and those around me.
- Follow through with what I said I would do every single time.

I would often ask myself, how can I release the thoughts that are trapped inside me, so that Christ in me, can overflow into the lives of others and bring forth the liberty in Christ I desire? Have you ever asked yourself this?

I have asked myself, why do I struggle to speak up and speak out? I felt that what I had to say was not valuable. I thought it would not be heard or accepted. I thought I was not good enough to pour into the lives of others. I had no self-belief. I had been fed lies of; you keep your mouth shut. You have no right to speak up or defend yourself, regardless, if you were right or wrong. I felt I had no voice for years. I felt that certain authorities or people who thought they were superior because they held a position or positions, therefore,

I felt I had no right to question their activities, or that something was wrong. Be truthful with yourself. Have you also felt this way at times?

I know the pain of false accusations, done in such a manipulative, passive aggressive manner that not even those that were supposed to have been able to sense it were able to; instead, my integrity and character were questioned. I do not blame them. I do not hold them responsible, because I know, and God knows, they did not and still do not know what I know about certain situations. They could not help me, simply because they did not understand. They did not see all the ins and outs of the matter or hear all the words spoken, but I rest in knowing God sees, hears, and knows all. Hebrews 4:12-13 "For the word of God is quick, and powerful, and sharper than any two-edged sword, piercing even to the dividing asunder of soul and spirit, and of the joints and marrow and is a discerner of the thoughts and intents of the heart. Neither is there any creature that is manifest in his sight: but all things are naked and opened unto the eyes of him with whom we must do,"

I know the pain of humiliation, belittlement amid superiors, and feeling less than who I am. My sense of confidence stripped away from me with each remark that had been made in such a way that left me feeling guilty for matters I should not have felt guilty about at all. Knowing that God knew the desires of my heart and that I love him more than life itself. I know the pain of being in imprisonment, as others went on living their lives as if nothing had happened. I was fed lies that my family would live a defeated life for the rest of our lives, and that we had no chance of being anything. I know the feeling of being controlled by people, their wants, their dreams, their desires to the point they will do what it takes to get where they want to be, even if it means trying to destroy you in the name of Jesus.

I know the feelings of being taken advantage of physically, mentally, emotionally, financially, and spiritually. I know the feelings of being misunderstood. I know a lonely journey with people all around me. Yet, it opened my eyes to the misunderstood journeys. If you are reading this book, I hope you can find healing in these words, as I did.

Chapter 1

A cry went out as word spread through the house that Joseph was a traitor. Like wildfire, words of damnation, deception, manipulation, and defeat went forth. Words so smoothly spoken, that as she held his robe in her hands, her words appeared to be true. Even the king was disappointed and had him thrown into prison.

Yes, maybe you have been wronged by others and are not able to find your voice to speak up for several reasons, such as, being told that no one would believe you because of who you are and who they are. I have lived years fighting fear of what others thought about me, because my integrity and character were demoralized. I feared and did not trust leadership, I felt angry at those that should have understood my situations or should have been spiritual enough to see through the scheme of words being so loosely thrown around. I was condemned in the eyes of many. Humiliated, deeply hurt, having relentless nightmares, crying uncontrollably, no one to talk to about these things (except to my Jesus), yet other accusers would appear and reappear thinking they knew the significant part. Trying to move on yet imprisoned in my own mind and heart. Asking myself, how could those you love be so cruel? How could those you are helping turn on you and make you feel so inadequate?

The king loved Joseph yet had him thrown in prison for deeds that were not his own. Joseph, while in prison, went through a process that only

God could help him with. The process that we all must walk through, forgiveness. It seems the king had forgotten about him. Oh, but timing is everything and God was preparing Joseph for greatness. A greatness so divine that he would feed the very ones that betrayed him as a child.

The king remembered him, and God brought forth deliverance in his family. Do you think that if Joseph had not kept a clean and righteous heart that God could have used him and exalted him when He did?

No. Therefore, it is detrimental for us, as God's children, to keep and protect our hearts during uncomfortable situations. We must decide what our response will be because the decisions we make affect not only ourselves, but everyone around us. We must guard our minds and hearts.

I remember having to fight through extremely negative thoughts, being desperately sick in every aspect of my being. I had nothing else to give. I was numb. I regretted not taking care of myself, thinking I was doing God a service. Oh, how I lacked wisdom. I had to ask God's forgiveness for not taking care of the temple He gave me. When we are weak in body and mind, the enemy will prey on us. He will use current and past hurts to plant seeds of hatred, bitterness, unforgiveness, and cause us to start blaming our own behaviors on others. We must never allow ourselves to get to this point. Blaming others never brings growth. You do not want to go there. It is this kind of thinking, which will cause us to become heart sick. We bring upon ourselves suffering. I had to learn to let go. I had to let them go quietly, yet it did not feel quiet at all. It is too painful holding on to people that God said your journey splits here. When we have served our purpose and God is ready to

turn the course of our journey. Do not fight it, trust Him.

We do not always see the path clearly. Sometimes our path can be thick with fog, we cannot see to take another step, we do not understand why the path is not clear, yet God orders our steps if we only trust Him. Pray for His grace to lead, guide, and direct our steps. We will meet people over our lifetime, but not everyone is meant to stay in our lives, they are only there for a season. We must understand that seasons are just as important. We will struggle to let go of certain people and it will seem easy for others, yet we must trust Jesus. His ways are above our ways. His thoughts above our thoughts. Isaiah 55:8 "For my thoughts are not your thoughts neither are your ways my ways, saith the Lord." God knows what is best for each one of us. Psalm 18:30 "As for God, His way is perfect: the word of the Lord is tried: He is a buckler to all those that trust in Him".

You may ask, "Why does she get downright vulnerable? Because I know that someone, now or later might gain strength from what I am able to share. God has a plan for everyone and His plan for me is to speak life experiences to help you get through, encourage, and bless you.

The fears that I dealt with for years were, what do others

think of me? What will they say? I feared not fitting in! I ask myself many times, "What happened to cause the distrust? "Life happened, mis-understandings, hurtful situations with no closure, and abusive, dictating, controlling leadership. We hold titles and positions, but this does not make us excellent leaders. Leaders are those that set the example and get in there with you.

Truth is, when I began to challenge myself to consider where I really stand with God, I was worried about the wrong things. True courage comes from fearing God and God alone. Then, things will line up as the will of God begins to flow as it is meant too. John 7:23 "He that believeth on me, as the scripture hath said, out of his belly shall flow rivers of living water." We are all human. God is God. People sometimes will try to hold others in bondage by reminding them of weeds in their lives. In turn, we waste too much time being loyal to our weeds, or tending the weeds of others, because of what others say, and miss God's blessings. Stop giving others control over your destiny!

As humans we try to put people in boxes and categorize who we think they are or who we want them to be, but God is clear about His expectations for each one of us! Be wise, be vigilant and follow God's own heart! You can want something as bad as the air you breath. Do not get discouraged, do not give up when it is not happening for you. Continue to be consistent and remember timing is everything! Be Intentional!

Write down your top three priorities for each day. Then, focus on how you will carry them out to reach your goal and fulfill your purpose!

1. Stop trying to fake it until you succeed.

2. Stop worrying about who accepts you or who does not. We cannot win them all!

3. Be authentic regardless.

4. Be thankful always.

God works in Mysterious ways, and He is faithful to those that seek Him in sincerity. He will work on our behalf if we are willing to follow his lead and hear His voice. "When a man's ways please the LORD, he maketh even his enemies to be at peace with him." Proverbs 16:7

Chapter 2

Certain man was going down from Jerusalem to Jericho, and he fell among robbers, who stripped him, beat him and left him for dead. As he left his house that day, he had no idea he would be robbed. As he lay there, let us just say the self-righteous came by and said, hmm, he must have deserved it and continued his way. We must beware not to fall into the trap of thinking we are better than the one lying on the ground. "Pride goeth before destruction, and a

haughty spirit before a fall."
Proverbs 16:18 "All the ways
of a man are clean in his own
eyes; but the Lord weigheth the
spirit" Proverbs 16:2.
Remember, "God is our refuge
and strength, a very present
help in trouble." Psalms 46:1.
God reminds us in Matthew 5:7
"Blessed are the merciful, for
they shall obtain mercy."

Now, here comes, (I am not
getting my hands dirty kind of
guy), he looks and walks on by.
I wonder what his thoughts
were that day. Something like,
ugh he is too much to deal

with, it will cost too much of my time and money to stop and help.

Then, came along a man that took in the situation, he did not care about the mess, he simply helped him. We do not know what happen that lead up to this man being taken advantage of, but it happened. The good Samaritan became the only chance that this beaten man had to survive and he did that which Jesus teaches us to do. Galatians 6:1 KJV "Brethren, if a man be overtaken in a fault, ye which are spiritual, restore such a one in the spirit of meekness; considering thyself, lest thou also be tempted." His actions remind me of the scripture when God saw His people in Jerusalem left for dead, He said in Ezekiel 16:6 "And when I passed by thee and saw thee polluted in thine own blood, I said unto thee when thou wast in thou blood, Live." When He sees us in our hardships, He wants to help us. He knows our name. He wants to save us from dying in a pit of sorrows.

We all go through times, when we get up in the morning and it seems everything is off. It can seem all is going wrong like this man that had been unjustly left to die. Hebrews 10:24–25, says, "And let us watch out for one another to provoke love and good works, not neglecting to gather together, as some do, but encouraging each other." This passage highlights two things we can do to help one another: to call forth and encourage. To call forth means to be called out and challenge others who are walking through this life with us, and to encourage them in their struggles. When one of my friends sees me slipping, she has the right to call out to me. When I am being impatient with my child, she can bring it to my attention. When I am not giving my child the benefit of the doubt, she can challenge me to look at it from a different perspective. When I am being impatient with life itself, she can encourage me, by reminding me that God has a purpose. She can offer sound advice. I want help. If I am the one that has been beaten down.

Please do not walk past me
thinking I am not worth it.

Sometimes the people we
thought friends, will come to
watch us, they will put wood
on the fire, step back and watch
us burn. Job's friends came and
watched him lose everything,
even his pride. They sat, seeing
him in the dust of his
unfortunate situation yet did
nothing to help him. I would
like to think that they did not
know how to help him. They
did not know what to say.

Most people have no clue
how to help someone.

Therefore, we should seek Christ and His principles so that we learn and live His ways, by fulfilling the examples He laid before us.

I met sleepless nights, weeping, understanding none of this madness that was happening in my life. Asking God, why? Tossing, turning, and finally falling asleep, only to be awakened by unnecessary nightmares that tormented me. I would pray out to God for His help, not knowing how to get through this. I would ask Him to cover me. Please God cover me with your presence, outside of your presence I cannot bear this pain. Please God, help me not to hate them, please God help me not to be angry. I would pray God help them, gritting my teeth in anger I would say help them. I do not want to pray for them right now, but God help them. I would fight through it until the anger subsided and I knew God had helped me break through. Then, the weeping again. Help me, God, was my everyday prayer and still is.

The process of guarding our heart is an intense one. We do not have to die in our wounded state of mind. God has a plan. "For I know the thoughts that I think towards you, saith the Lord, thoughts of peace, and not of evil, to give you an expected end." Jeremiah 29:11

We fight not against flesh and blood, but against demonic powers and spirits that will attach themselves to those that allow him space. If we are not praying, if we are entertaining evil thoughts about one another, if we are jealous or envious of others, Satan will take his leap, step inside and deceive us into believing that we are walking uprightly before God, while being used to complete one of his many malicious tasks. The story about Paul comes to mind before he was converted. He mistreated and hurt believers before God opened his eyes and allowed him to see his cruel ways. He thought he was doing the right thing in the name of the law, yet he was way off course. Christians fall into this trap, because the truth be known, many of us are self-righteous and think we can do no wrong. We think that his tactics are only for the sinner. We are all sinners, shaped in iniquity. For these reasons we must know God's word, apply them, and write them on our hearts, believe them and hold on to them, this part is hard, and our soul depends on them. Ephesians 6:11 "Put on the whole armour of God, that ye may be able to stand against the wiles of the devil." Do not dare let him play with your mind. "For the night is far spent, the day is at hand: let us therefore cast off the works of darkness and let us put on the armour of light." Romans 13:12

Healthy relationships do not look like what we see from a show on television or social media, because real friends are those who get down in the trenches of life with you. They do not just call us out when we need calling out; they also encourage us by being there, praying over our fears and worries, and holding our hand when nothing makes sense. We should do the same for them. Encouraging one another should never be a chore. It should be something we do from the abundance of our heart. It can be showing up with an encouraging word. It can be delivering flowers. It can be sending a card in the mail. It can be as simple as a text to say you are thinking of your friend.

The accountability we experience when we are in genuine unity allows us to help one another move forward and deeper in relationship with the Lord. It is our responsibility to motivate and inspire one another to encourage each other to be the people God wants! When we allow ourselves to become open to genuine friendships, we find God's Word lived out, right before us. And yes, genuine, biblical relationships are hard to come by, but they do still exist.

When we have honest friends, who push us to be more and encourage us in our weaknesses, we grow and become better. We are courageous people looking out for our families and only want the best for them. We must always keep this in our focus. Remember, always lift one another up in prayer! We never know what someone else may be facing.

Chapter 3

During our process of forgiveness, "Be not overcome with evil, but overcome evil with good." Romans 12:21. We do not need to scream from the roof tops all the wrongs done, we do not need to blame those that hurt us, we do not need to talk bad about them, we do not need to slander them. There were times I wanted to scream everything I know from the house tops, but I did not, even when it was said that I did. I rest in the beautiful fact that Jesus knows all. We Must Pray

Hard to Protect Our House, Our Souls Depend on It!

Remember, they laughed as they spit on Him, mocked Him, and asked Him if He was really the King of the Jews, He was silent. Jesus was placed in the tomb for three days, but He rose on the third day, the Truth prevailed. We need silence, a place to think, a place to steal away until the troubled waters are settled. I had to step away. I stepped away to a place in which I call my haven. I was so divided, and it hurt hard to take this step, yet it was a place where I could pull my thoughts together, a place in which I could live for Jesus, sort things out in my mind and soul, a place of healing. I was able to heal without the chaos breathing down my neck. I thank God for patient men and women that knew nothing and still know nothing about my hurtful situations, but were there for me, my husband, and our children.

When the highest King says enough is enough and you have proven yourself faithful throughout the process, regardless, if man feels you have or not, He steps in and gives you that refreshing drink and carries you to a dimension of faith that only He can. He brings you out of the prison and breaks the chains that have tried to bind you. He calls you forth into your destiny, will bless you with more than you had before. Raise you up to prove His righteousness and His glory does not go unseen.

What was meant for evil against Jesus, was exactly Gods will, to redeem the souls of men. What was meant to harm you and I, must be turned into a determination to live above defeat because through Jesus we are victorious. There is only one that is defeated and that is the enemy of our souls. His destiny was already decided when he was cast out of heaven. Jesus gave His life, went into hell, and took back the keys to death, hell and the grave.

We have the keys to defeat any obstacle that would try to block our way. One of those keys is the choice to choose our response. Will I remain defeated because someone said I would always be defeated, or will I take Jesus at His Word and trust that I am more than a conqueror and that "I can do all things through Christ which strengthens me." Philippians 4:13? No one has the right to choose our destiny, but God and our right to choose to live above the negative words lashed at us.

I heard this one morning while doing my devotions. Someone calls out, Hey Stupid! And YOU turn around. Then YOU get upset at that person.

But YOU are the one who
responded by turning around to
acknowledge what they said.
Remember, that is their
opinion, not your reality. Stop
turning around. Stop
acknowledging and thinking
you are what others say of you.
Know who God wants you to
be, acknowledge Him, focus on
His truths, and let others
opinionated words drop dead
where they are. Do not allow
their negative world to
penetrate yours. Stop
responding negatively. The
load will get lighter. The
weight will begin to fall off

piece by piece. I wish that I would have learned this lesson much quicker than I did. But what relief I feel now! Love, joy, peace, confidence and more positives will replace it. "Peace I leave with you, my peace I give unto you: not as the world giveth, give I unto you. Let not your heart be troubled, neither let it be afraid." John 14:27 KJV

What words are we speaking into our lives, the lives of our children, the lives of those we meet daily? Our words can free us or hold us hostage. When we believe and speak the wrong words, we will feel hopeless. Proverbs 6:2 "Thou art snared with the words of thy mouth." Stop speaking words of fear, start speaking words of faith. Mark 9:23 "If thou canst believe, all things are possible..." When God spoke, His words became what He declared. He wants us to be His followers. John 14:12 "He that believeth on me, the works that I do, shall he do also." This is powerful. Matthew 16:19 "I give you the keys to the Kingdom, whatever you bind on earth is bound in heaven. We have the power, which is the Holy Ghost, within us to overcome negativity.

Remember that God's Word is forever settled in heaven. Psalm 119:89. His words are already proven. He said that He will not break his own covenant, nor alter a thing that was spoken from His mouth. Psalm 89:34 We are set into action by our words. For life or death is in our tongue. Will we speak words of life or words of death?

We try hard to forgive, we pray, we quote scriptures, we

sing, and we start feeling good and think, it is over, I have overcome, I have forgiven them. Suddenly, something is said, or you see someone and all the hurt floods back in.

Forgiveness is a heart cleanser. It releases the oppressed feelings of hurt in our lives. It frees the soul! Yes, we get hurt. We have also hurt others; we are not above anyone in making this mistake. No one has been any more hurt than Jesus Christ. Jesus cried, "Father, forgive them, for they know not what they do." You may say, well, He was God, therefore, it was easy for Him. Stop, using this line as an excuse to hold on to your hate. His spirit was strong and said, "Thy will be done", yet his flesh cried out, "Father, if it be thy will, let this cup pass from me."

Do we really want deliverance? Do we want peace? We are the ones that MUST make up our minds that we are done wallowing in the murky, stickiness of those things that keep us bound. We must decide if we really want healing. We, with God's help are the writer of our own STORY. Our response decides the outcome of our fate.

Will it be love, joy, and peace, even when storms arise? Will our response be to give it to God, or hold it? Will it be, to continue in our self-righteousness, believing we are Godly; knowing our heart needs cleansed?

You might ask, how can I defeat this fear and worry that tries to creep into my life? Declare Gods Word and speak to them aloud every time you feel fear or worry about circumstances. "Ye are of God, little children, and have overcome them: because greater is He that is in you, than He that is in the world." I John 4:4 "I will fear no evil for thou art with me, Thy rod and Thy staff comforted me." Psalm 23:4 Choose scriptures to post on our mirror, refrigerator, in our car, etc. Learn them, use these scriptures to fight off the spirits of fear and other situation that we need reassurance with.

I remember as a little girl, I was afraid of the dark, and I would have nightmares. My momma told me to put my Bible under my pillow or hold it until I fell asleep. She taught me to pray over myself. Jesus, I plead your blood over my sleep and my dreams tonight. Protect me as I sleep. Thank you, Amen. I did this for years and it worked. As a child, momma was teaching me simple faith. As I grew, other fears and life occurrences happened and I had to learn to have faith in God through each situation in a different depth, but God will honor our faith no matter the depth of our faith.

Once we choose to stop carrying the weight of unforgiveness, hate, bitterness, we lay the conditions of our heart at the feet of Jesus and quit blaming everyone for the response to choose to carry these heavy burdens, healing will come!

"No weapon formed against you shall prosper; and every tongue that shall rise against thee in judgement thou shalt condemn. This is the heritage of the servants of the

Lord, and their righteousness is of Me, saith the Lord." There are so many more words from God that we can speak during every situation of our lives.

"There shall no evil befall me, neither any plague come near my dwelling, for He shall give His angels charge over me, to keep me in all my ways." Psalms 91:10-11 Speak words of life and freedom over yourself, your family, your household, your workplaces, those you are around daily, and speak over your situation. We are more than conquerors in Christ Jesus.

You may ask, why are you so bold about this subject? My answer to you is, I know the pain of hurt, hate, bitterness, and the blame game. I also know liberty in mind, spirit, and soul. It is a freedom like no other. Christ love in me did and still does help me forgive every single day! It is a working process. I am not perfect by no means, but allowing God to guide me, is what helps me get through.

We must edify one another in love. The edification of our faith takes place within the church (I'm not referring to a mere building, but we as a body of people coming together in one mind and one accord), the manifestation of our faith takes place as we live our lives on an everyday basis, the places we go, the people we meet, our attitudes in which we present on every level of our lives.

Are we genuinely edifying one another in love as the unified church? Is God truly being

manifest in our everyday
lifestyle? Can a seed of life be
planted through our words and
actions as our day plays out
before us? I recall making a
phone call to one of my
creditors. I was struggling
financially and wanted to see
what we could work out in
terms of getting back on track.
The conversation switched
from business to personal as
Michelle and I began to share
each other's struggles over the
past few months and how that
God has been faithful through
it all. By the time we hung up
the phone we had connected in

a way that I would have never thought when I initially picked up the phone. We both needed encouragement and were able to help one another. I had commented that I wish there were a way we could still stay in contact, but due to confidentiality she was not allowed to give any information except for her first name. A week later, I received a box on my doorstep. When I opened the box, it was a gorgeous African Lillies plant from Michelle. This is how seeds of encouragement are planted. Being a living

testimony is what God expects
of us.

Chapter 4

The word integrity continues to roll over and over in my mind. It is the quality of being honest and having strong moral principles, moral uprightness. Having integrity means that we live in agreement with our deepest values, we are honest with ourselves and with others, and we keep our word. Integrity is a valued character trait. Another meaning for integrity is the state of being whole and undivided.

Integrity brings together honesty (telling the truth), being open (transparent), not taking advantage of others, trust, pride, and helping others.

How do we show integrity?

1. Keep our word.
   A. If we want to prove a solid reputation, we must keep our promises.
   B. Keep our commitments.
   C. Take responsibility for our own actions.
2. Pay attention to our environment.
   A. Stay focused.

B. Surround ourselves with honest people.

C. Respect one another.

Integrity is a trait that is slowly fading away. We must hold dear our principles and integrity. Integrity is being honest with yourself, even when you are alone. Honesty is being truthful with others. The Bible says, many shall be deceived and walk in their own ways, but He leads the path of the righteous. Matt 24; Pro 8:20

What does Jesus think about our integrity? Are we

truly walking the path of integrity or are we being deceived?

The scripture clearly says," Be not deceived for God is NOT mocked." "Seek ye therefore His righteousness." We turn our face from Him when we most need Him and would rather compromise salvation of souls to appease our pride and live out what others think of us instead of being who we truly are. Yet, it does not have to be this way. We must choose to cry out in prayer, for His grace and mercy. Let the souls rise, we must let our voices be heard for the salvation of many. Our actions and integrity in how we respond to our circumstances, hardships and wellbeing is essential to the soul. Through life's experiences others can relate and be saved by seeing the faithfulness of ones living testimony. Does it make it right, the hurts caused? No, but to have freedom, we must surrender the situation to God.

Put God first, in all things, be grateful, make meaningful connections. Unity brings forth power. Helping others is empowering. Our connection with others matters. We must be committed, diligent, and intentional in every action taken!

Do we know Him and hold within our heart His knowledge, like we say we do? Let us take time to think on these things and truthfully answer these questions within ourselves. Let us train ourselves to speak God's Word. Ephesians 5:1 reads "to be followers of God, as dear children..." Children want to imitate those they love, especially their dad and mom. We must follow God as a child does his/her father. We will walk like Him, talk like Him, speak words of faith and much more. We must be about our father's business!

Chapter 5

Day after day her element became worse. She went to every physician possible and still no positive result to share. Her body continued to decline, and she felt hopeless. I cannot imagine the pain she felt and the mockery she received while carrying this illness of an issue of blood. Yet, what strikes my curiosity is that she continued to seek help, she was consistent in finding a solution, yet had found none. What pushed her to her destiny? What drove her to keep reaching for help? She never stopped trying. How great was her faith? She would not give in; she would not quit. I would like to think that Jesus intentionally went where she could see Him and the crowd passing by on purpose to fulfil His purpose in her life that day. Even in her weakening state, being pushed away, glared at, stepped on, she did not cease to make her way to Jesus. As hard as it was, she pressed. Her faith was so great, she just wanted to touch him. As she came closer, she began to fall, reaching, as she fell, her fingers reached out to touch the hem of His garment. Oh, what virtue, what beauty as she lay on the ground that day surrounded by people, Jesus stopped and said, "Who touched me?" We know that Jesus knows all things, so why did He ask the question. The disciples said, Jesus the crowd is great, and you ask who touched you. Everyone is touching you, but Jesus knew that there was a faith greater than all those surrounding Him, He said, "Virtue has left my body". That day she received healing and blessings because she touched Him through her persistence, her willingness to seek Him no matter the cost. Her faith propelled her to keep going. If I can just touch Him. If I can just touch Him.

Jesus has redeemed us all from the curse of the law. We can pray and plead His blood over our bodies when we are sick. Eph. 6:16 tells us that we can take the shield of faith and quench every fiery dart that the wicked one brings against us. Romans 8:11 tells us that if God's spirit lives in us, then he can quicken our mortal bodies by His spirit, just as he raised up Christ from the dead.

I would pray God, please let me raise my babies. God, they need to know you. I began to search God's word for scriptures about healing. I would pray that He would deliver me from the infirmities that I felt.

I was not one to share my personal difficulties, because I did not want to be mistaken for complaining and I do not want pity. For years I would have sugar drops to the point that they said I should have been in coma. But GOD!

Finally, able to get help in that area, but continued to have horrible left side sensations of pain, weakness, not able to move like I should, then I was told I was having TIA's (mini strokes) fatigued, weak, dizzy, headaches, But GOD!

Now, on to figuring out why the TIAs. In 2019 they found a small hole in my heart, in which I have lived with my entire life. But GOD.

I struggled with my health in ways, most people have no idea. From doctor to doctor, then on to specialists, in and out of E.R. trying to figure out why I felt the way I did. I

I had to work through the fears, tears and my body completely doing what It wanted without my mental permission, But GOD.

Through it all, my faith has become deeper than ever before. I worried about what others thought about me. I was told I was faking numerous times; I was told I was unfaithful to God due to missing church services, because of lack of understanding on their part, but the truth is, faithfulness goes much deeper than many want to know about because it cost something. Even through the mental part of it, I would go to God's Word and read what He thinks about me. At times I have felt that I have missed so much. Tears would flow down my face as I laid on the couch or bed unable to get up and school my children. Unable to go to church service after service. Unable to fully function the way I know I'm suppose too. It would hurt to hear my children say, "you're always sick, why can't you take us to the park, why can't we do this or that?" I would try to explain the best I could. My kids saw my daddy come and pick me up to take me to ER with stroke like symptoms or having a full-blown kidney stone trying to pass, while my husband was at work. They also saw when my momma would come and help with them and take care of me while I lay crying in bed because I did not want to be a burden to them. They saw the times I cried out to God to heal me, so that I could function on a normal level.

Here is a prayer that I pray over myself when I am feeling ill. "God, you created my body, you know every fiber, every cell, every detail. You know exactly what is causing the pain or the health issues. Cover me with your blood. Now, body or (the specific issue) call it out loud, come under subjection to the authority and power of God's Word "For He was wounded for my transgression, He was bruised for my iniquities, the chastisement of my peace was upon Him, and with His stripes I am healed" Is. 53:5. (personalize His words in your mouth and speak them into existence). "Heal me, O Lord, and I shall be healed; save me, and I shall be saved: for Thou art my praise." Jer. 17:14 Remind your body that Jesus healed all manner of sickness and disease. He is the same yesterday, today and forever. What He did then, He can do now! We may ask God, why don't we see your power like they did? God has all power to do anything, but we must believe, have faith without wavering.

This scripture can be prayed during spiritual sickness and battles too. When the spirit is weak, the enemy will try to set traps, but we must be wise and be on the lookout for his wicked snares, so we do not fall into them.

Our mindset of doubt ties His hands at fulfilling His promises. He said, ask and ye shall receive. He asks, believe ye that I can do this? They said, yes Lord. That is when, He touched their eyes and said, "According to YOUR FAITH be it unto you." Matthew 9:28

Take Him at his word, speak His words, and be made whole! It is not God's will for us to lack anything. Ps. 23:1 "The Lord is my Shephard; I shall not want." Phil. 4:19 "But my God shall supply all your needs according to His riches in glory by Christ Jesus." Matthew 21:22 "And all things, whatsoever ye shall ask in prayer, believing, ye shall receive."

James 4: 2-3 "You have not because you ask not."

Psalm 37:4 "Delight thyself in the Lord and he shall give you

the desires of your heart."
Remember to ask, but faith
without works is dead. Ask,
believe, act upon your faith,
and receive. Proverbs 4:20-22
"attend unto my words...they
are life and health to all flesh."
We complicate things, but it
really is that simple!!!

Chapter 6

Life can be unpredictable. Yes, it can change you. Life can challenge you. It can throw hard curve balls when you least expect it. It can shake you to your core. Life happens to every single soul. Yet, life is a journey. It can take us places high or low. It can teach us if we allow it. But the most important thing about life is knowing the voice of God. Sometimes He will speak to us in that still small voice, in the quiet of the night. Sometimes it is in a vision or in a dream.

Sometimes He speaks to us while praying and other times through another person that He chooses to use. Sometimes while reading scriptures He will jump out at us and really make us think. Sometimes His words are tough to take, yet it is His love for us, that speaks. Sometimes He speaks through the storms, His voice like the thunder, His actions like the lightning bolts, yet the rain brings such soothing, knowing it refreshes and washes us clean. Sometimes He speaks through the means of glistening white snow, and the birds that

He sends our way to enjoy, as He feeds them. Sometimes He is silent, as we ponder Him and His Glory. However, He may be speaking, we must know our Father's voice and follow Him.

Is God unchangeable? Yes, God never changes. (Psalm 33:11)

In darkness, He is our Light. (John 8:12)

In sickness, He is our healer. (I Peter 2:24)

In grief, He is our comfort. (2 Cor. 1:3-4)

In tears, He is our joy. (Zeph 3:17)

In lack, He is our provider. (Matt. 33:34)

In tough times, He is our refuge. (Psalm 46:1)

In addictions, He is our deliverer. (Psalm 18:2)

In persecution, He is the shelter to run to. (Psalm 27:5)

In fear, He is with us. (Isaiah 41:10)

In battle, He raises a stand against him. (Isaiah 59:19)

In chaos, He is the calm in the raging storm. (Psalm 107:29)

In death, He is eternal life. (Psalm 48:14)

In saving, He redeems us. (Psalm 23:3)

In prayer, He bonds with us. (Matt. 11:28-30)

In worship, He blesses us. (Ex. 23:25)

In praise, He strengthens us. (Psalm 150:6) (Joshua 1:9)

In Thanks, He pours his love on us. (I Chr. 16:34)

In love, He wraps us in His loving care. (1 Pet. 5:7)

In Faith, He acts on our behalf. (Pro. 3:5-6)

In persistence, He gives us hope. (Ps.138:3)

In Discipline, He becomes our lifestyle. (Ps. 1:1-6)

In relationship, He becomes that solid foundation. (1 Cor. 2:9-10)

In Life, He is my Rock. (Matthew 7:24-27)

Jesus said, upon this rock, I will build my church. (Matt. 16:18)

Each day that we mature in Him, the Rock becomes stronger, our faith grows, our trust in Him gets deeper. The foundation cannot be broken. Restoration for our soul is in Him

I ask myself the question, "Am I willing to pay the price to rise up and be a part of His church as He intends it to be?

When I began to think on these things, I cannot help myself. I must share with you, His goodness. And His praise shall continuously be in my mouth. (Psalm 34:1)

Chapter 7

We have asked, Is God a respecter of persons? Romans 2:11 "For there is no respect of persons with God." People all over the world seek God. You might say, but what about:

Abraham he was a friend of God. (John 15:13)

Noah walked in Obedience. (Genesis 6)

David was a man after God's own heart. (1 Sam. 13:14)

Daniel walked with God. (The book of Daniel)

Mary Magdalene was a loyal follower of Jesus. (Mark 15:40)

Rahab recognized the one true God. (Joshua 2)

Ruth decided to serve the God of Naomi. (The book of Ruth)

There are more we could add, but all these people had one thing in common, they all made mistakes, yet they were true worshippers of God! God does not seek class, He seeks a relationship with all men, women, and children. He seeks true worshippers and prayer warriors.

But we are too busy tripping over the decisions that others make for their own lives and seeing the negative side of their fall that we say, well, I cannot live for God because David committed adultery, then had a man killed to hide his sin. If we will not live for God, because we do not like another person's path, then we are the ones with the heart issue. We must stop basing our relationship with God on what others do and how they live their lives. If we are doing this, we live a very shallow life. We do not believe that God is a just God and are not giving God our best. If we struggle to line up, because we think someone else does not line up then our own priorities are messed up. Give God our whole heart, pray for others and feel the change. Seek God and lean not to our own understanding. Later, down the road David suffered the consequences of his decisions. Did God bring it upon him? No, he brought it upon himself. But David repented before God. David was indeed a man after God's own heart. God forgave him.

We must wake up, rise
and be the example of change
that we want to see around us,
but do not dare point fingers
and word blast others. As we
pray for others around us, pray
also, create in me a clean heart,
o God, renew within me a right
spirit. God, help us to always
keep our priorities in the paths
of righteousness for You are
righteous.Therefore, I could not
and never want to live without
Jesus! He is the Deliverer, Way
Maker, the only one who
utterly understands the heart.

For nothing is impossible for God! We are more than overcomers in Him!!!

Ps. 24:7 "Lift up your heads, o ye gates, and be ye lifted up, ye everlasting doors, and the King of Glory shall come in." For nothing is impossible for God! "A thousand may fall at your side and ten thousand at thy right hand, but it shall not come near you" Psalms 91:7. We are more than overcomers in Him!!!

Chapter 8

Sometimes we think we know what someone else is going through, we think we know the depth of their faith, we think we see the entire story, but we only see what that person allows us to see. Sometimes we judge a person by what we think of them and by what little bit we see, but if we would allow God to use us, be led by Him, and have compassion, things could be revealed in a different light. I feel it will give hope to others that sometimes feel hopeless and weary. God never leaves us, nor forsakes us. He is faithful in every situation if we allow Him to be. Singing and praising Jesus helped me through many days. Therefore, I love Him so much!!! Throughout my process of healing, I would feel like a failure. Failure has a different meaning for different people. It is a means of learning what does not work and keep trying until successful. Someone might look at failure as a steppingstone to achieving more by learning valuable lessons of always getting back up, dust off and persevere. Others refuse to allow failure to dictate their destiny, they allow their mistakes and falls to push them to a level of higher achievements and goals. Some people allow the fear of failure to stop them in their tracks to the point that they never take that risk of trying. Others hate failures, because they think it puts them in a certain category of not being good enough. Sometimes people fear failures because they are afraid of how others will perceive them. Failure to others means criticism and rejection. We hate the feeling of not being accepted by those around us. The truth about failure is that it cannot decide your destiny! YOU have the choice to learn from the falls or to give in to the falls. Trying, failing, and getting back up is so beautiful! Failing is a part of the process of overcoming fears that we face head on. We will become stronger each time we choose to learn from our trying and failing experiences. Michael Jordan had the game winning shot in his hands 947 times. He made 146 of those winning shots. That means he missed over seven hundred shots. Did that keep him from trying repeatedly? NO! Because he understood the value of the process. Try, fail, try, fail, Win!!! He did not allow his losses to decide his wins!!! He was determined to win. Thinking back, I remember as my dad worked hard to provide for a family of 10. He did so many different things to make ends meet. It took him years to achieve what he has achieved today. I was having a rough time and he came to me and said, "Sis, you must keep digging them wells just like

Isaac did, when the enemy would fill them back up, he would dig another well. You must keep moving, keep digging, never give up." I will never forget his words, because he was speaking from experience. I watched him do the same. How we respond to losses decides the wins we will achieve! Become determined to face the fear of failure, take that risky step to freedom, when you fall, dust yourself off and learn from that fall. Keep stepping towards your victory. Growth will happen. As growth happens you will become stronger in the face of adversity. Always remember, no matter how much we feel we know, there is always more to learn. Learn to learn from every experience and keep stepping forward!!! Never give up; keep pushing forward with everything you have. Inspire others, even in your storm, it will help you move forward! Take 15-20 minutes a day to sit and think. Write your thoughts on paper, this helps clear your mind and make room for new thoughts. Pray about these things that you feel hold you back and give it to God. We must allow Him space in our thoughts to order our steps as He wants for our lives. Here is something else that I have found that helps, when everything feels like it is going wrong, to the point of frustration, take 5-15 minutes to process it, cry if you need too. Then, ask yourself, "Will this matter in 30 minutes, will it matter tomorrow, will this matter a year from now?" If you can say, no, then pull out that smile and choose to LET IT GO!!!

Chapter 9

I read this story a while ago it talked about a group of boys that were out hiking one day when they stumbled upon an old, abandoned railroad track. One of the boys tried walking the rail. After taking his first steps he lost his balance and fell. Another boy tried and fell. The others laughed. He hollered out, "I bet you can't do it either." One by one they all tried and failed. Then, two boys began whispering to each other. One of them challenged the others:

"I can walk all the way to the end, and so can he." "No, you can't," the other boys that had tried and failed said. "Bet you a candy bar each we can!" He said, the boys accepted. They both hopped onto a rail, reached out an arm, locked hands with the other, and carefully walked the entire distance. Sometimes we cannot meet the challenge alone but working together we can.

How can I teach my children and others how to be successful people in every aspect of life, if I have not set the example? How can I share my testimony if I have no faith in God? How can I understand pain, and help others through it, if I have not walked through pain? How can I financially bless others if I haven't any to give? How can I share my time with others if I have no time to spare? My mentor, has always told me, "You must become selfish, so that you can become unselfish." To become someone that can help others, you must first help yourself.

When my family travels to Brazil, one of the things they

tell us is, if the oxygen mask fall, always put yours on first, so you can help your children or someone else near. Why? Because if you pass out, you will not be a help to anyone. My WHY is bigger than me and it includes you!!! I had no idea the possibilities that were at arm's length, until I went through life's experiences and needed to trust in God for my very existence; something we do not even think about. We breathe and think nothing of it, yet each breath is God- given. With God anything is possible.

Flowers do not grow and
bloom over night, but when
they bloom, Oh, the beauty!
And remember, butterflies were
not always a beautiful butterfly,
they went through their process
and came out magnificent!!!

Chapter 10

Bound by the chains and shackles, imprisoned by my own insecurities, hurts, pains at no fault of my own, yet I must figure a way out of this. Being in this prison of hurts is not for me. I must pray my way out of these wretched chains and heavy bondage of negative feelings and thoughts. I cannot stay in this state, for if I do, I will die. In prison, we do not eat like we would at home, we do not sleep well, we have no way of getting a warm hot shower any time we want, we are at the mercy of those that control us. I will NOT die a death of defeat. As I look around, shoulder to shoulder with other prisoners, I thought to myself we all need help, we all need delivered. In this prison of bondage, we need a supernatural power to save us. It cannot be done on our own. That is when I made up my mind no one person will ever control my destiny by keeping me bound in a disgusting prison of self-pity. I decided that God will deliver me so that I can help other prisoners around me to escape this nasty forbidden place. Yes, we are all hurt from time to time, but we must choose to allow God to teach us through it. Be moldable, learn from our pain instead of squirming in it and feeling sorry for ourselves. Remember, we have people all around us that are watching our example. The difference from getting over what people do to hurt us and being that example for those that are watching is that God gets glorified when one can allow Him to heal them during the process of being imprisoned, being in solitude, being in an unhealthy situation, being put in the fire to become someone stronger in Christ. There is something powerful about unified prayer for one another, for those that have gone astray and for those that do not believe yet. Acts 12 talks about when Peter, a disciple of God, was thrown into prison for doing God's work. While he was in his (what looked like) weakened state, he prayed. Even, though his situation looked impossible, nothing is impossible with God. Acts 12:5 "Peter therefore was kept in prison: but prayer was made without ceasing of

the church unto God for him."
Who interceded for him? The
Church, people like you and
me. Suddenly, an angel was
before him, and the prison was
filled with light. The angel
spoke to Peter, "Arise up
quickly." And his chains fell
off him. The angel said, get up,
put on your shoes, pull yourself
together and follow me. Peter
obeyed! As he followed the
angel, he thought he was
having a vision, yet he was
being delivered of his current
unfortunate situation. When
Peter realized that he was
indeed set free, he went to the

house of Mary, mother of John, and began to knock. The very ones that had been praying for his deliverance were also the ones that had a tough time believing that it was really Peter. God works in mysterious ways. This way He receives the glory for the deliverance. We pray for things and when God answers them, we act shocked that God really came through and brought deliverance. We lack so much faith. God's promises are true, can you image what it would be like if we would only believe and take hold of them as He wants. We must stop imagining and put His promises into action by the obedience of His words, backed by our faith. We must get up, put on our shoes of faith and garments of praise, and obey as He leads us out of life's difficulties. And if He chooses not to remove us from certain trials of life, He will go through it with us. The three Hebrew boys are prime examples for not being taken out of their situation. They had to go through the fire for God's power to be manifest and His glory to be known by the king and all those involved in that

situation. He also built the faith
of the three Hebrew boys by
showing up in the hottest most
fiery part of their trial. It is in
the fire that we are purified, we
can become cleansed and
formed into the most precious
jewels. We grow strength that
only God can give. When we
do come forth as beautiful
diamonds, and God has started
a work in us that no man can
take credit for. That is when
humanity stands in awe and
says, was not he/she the one
that was left for dead as an
outcast as everyone walked
past, except one. Did not such

and such say this about them. I
thought they were a lost cause.
I thought there was no escape. I
thought they would never
amount to anything, yet God is
so faithful to those that choose
to reach for His help. "If my
people who are called by my
name will humble themselves
and pray, I will heal their land."
My interpretation is, if my
people that love me and
humble themselves (admit that
they need help) and cry out in
my name, I will heal their
minds, hearts, souls.

Just because you get delayed, does not mean you will not get there! He wants to start a new thing in each one of us. I John 2:8 "Again, a new commandment I write unto you: because the darkness is past, and the true light now shineth." Be true to your now, not your then. Stop giving fear a place to live yet continue in Godly fear (A Respect for God). We must step into our purpose. My steps are ordered by the Lord, always have been, and always will be. "As for me and my house, we will serve the Lord."

Step up to the fearless leader that you are in Christ; a leader with determination, a leader that knows humility yet allows God to lead the way to the destiny He wants for us. He will never lead us in the wrong direction. Be confident in God because before we knew ourselves, He already knew us.

Jeremiah 1:5 "Before I formed you in the womb, I knew you."

I Corinthians 6:20 "For ye are bought with a price: therefore, glorify God in your body, and your spirit, which are God's."

In Gods eyes we are worth saving.

STOP LOOKING BACK! That is an old story. Write a new one in Christ!!!

Affirmation Scriptures

Ephesians 4:32 "And be ye kind one to another, tenderhearted, forgiving one another, even as God for Christ's sake hath forgiven you."

Jeremiah 30:17 "For I will restore your health unto thee, and I will heal thee of thy wounds, saith the Lord; because they called thee an outcast, saying, this is Zion, whom no man seeketh after."

Joel 2:25-26 "And I will restore to you the years that the locust hath eaten, the cankerworm, and the caterpillar, and the palmerworm, my great army which I sent among you. And ye shall eat in plenty, and be satisfied, and praise the name of the Lord your God, that hath dealt wondrously with you: and my people shall never be ashamed."

About the Author

Charity Siqueira is the second of eight children, raised in a small town in Southern Illinois. She is a wife and mom of two. God and her family are her first priorities.

Charity assisted on the mission field in the country of Brazil for nearly 12 years. Her passion was and is to empower and encourage those near and afar. She is a kind, caring soul that loves God and hopes to inspire her readers to seek God in every circumstance in life.

During her journey through forgiveness, healing and restoration she felt she could help others through the process of forgiveness by writing down and sharing her story. Connect with her by sending an email:

beinspired@hopeblessingspublication.com

References:

Holy Bible, King James Version referenced

The Boys and the Railroad Metaphor - Author Unknown

The Name Calling metaphor- Author Unknown

God's Creative Power - Charles Capps